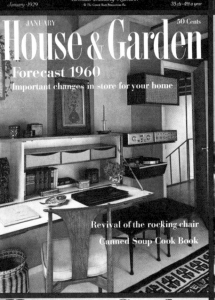

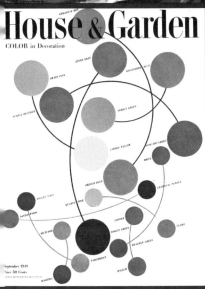

THE Well-LIVED LIFE

© 2003 Assouline Publishing, Inc.

Assouline Publishing, Inc.
601 West 26th Street
18th floor
New York, NY 10001
USA
Tel.: 212 989-6810   Fax: 212 647-0005

www.assouline.com

ISBN: 2 84323 445 X

Color separation: Gravor (Switzerland)
Printing: Grafiche Milani (Italy)

ONE HUNDRED YEARS OF HOUSE & GARDEN

Dominique Browning
and The Editors of House & Garden Magazine

THE Well-LIVED LIFE

ASSOULINE

Contents

Foreword

Few magazines can lay claim to a century of history, or to having published images by so many extraordinary and distinguished photographers, among them Alfred Eisenstaedt, Horst P. Horst, André Kertész, Paul Strand, Irving Penn, and John Rawlings. *The Well-Lived Life: One Hundred Years of House & Garden* is a chronicle not just of a periodical but, more important, of a country and a culture coming into its own. We drew lessons from the places, especially Europe, and times that shaped our tastes, but fashioned something bold, something that was and is unmistakably, uniquely American.

We have organized this book into eight chapters, beginning with Interior Drama, which reflects the growing confidence and imagination reflected in American interiors. Pride of Place examines the changing definition of home, the innumerable ways we make a house a mirror of ourselves. Domestic Bliss focuses on the quotidian routines of home life, of children and dogs, cars and dishwashers, and on the magazine's mission to help readers run their households smoothly, especially in decade after decade of enormous social change. Garden Design surveys the variegated landscape of our green, growing spaces, from rigid formality to wild, blowsy beauty. Outdoor Living illuminates the joys, sedentary or sporting, we always have found outside our back doors, and Flowers takes a close look at blooms, from the humble to the rare, and their ability to charm, seduce, amaze, and inspire. Entertaining revels in the dinners, picnics, clambakes, teas, and parties of a country that has dedicated itself to welcoming others. Finally, Home Away from Home travels to the places we build to get away from it all, the cabins, cottages, and summer palaces where we shed the formality and stress of everyday life. For all their variety, these chapters have a common bond, the abiding affection for how and where we make our lives.

Interior Drama

Americans used to have a walloping inferiority complex about Europe. Magazines about domestic life at the turn of the twentieth century gave readers tips on where to find chateaux, manors, and villas that well-heeled readers could import, stone by stone, from Spain, Italy, Germany, France, or England. By 1910, however, it was apparent that Americans interested in the arts of living well were far less likely to castle-shop or use their houses as repositories for grand tour artifacts (oh, those elephant-foot umbrella stands!). Instead, they were building elegant houses from the ground up (some according to architects' plans purchased from magazines) and decorating them as they chose. Articles on furniture and gardening began to appear alongside those on architectural styles. As a result, the publications known as shelter magazines quickly became the means for disseminating a uniquely American point of view on design. Editors sent photographers everywhere to record evolving trends in architecture and interiors. Readers, freed from the constraints of turning their homes into models of verisimilitude to styles of other times and places, were encouraged to indulge themselves, and to experiment—with extravagant pieces of furniture, bold wallpapers, imaginative window treatments, and unusual props.

Probably the twentieth century's greatest interior drama, one still playing to packed houses, is the not-so-genteel conflict—though some might call it a sofa opera—between so-called traditional decoration and so-called modern design. Like savvy impresarios, as soon as the first curve was straightened, the magazines, like the chorus of a Greek tragedy, began limning the battle pitched between what was then called, and what is still called, "good taste" and the brash, stripped-down stylistic bravado of brave new machine-age designs.

Let's say, for the sake of argument, that the drama opened at the Exposition des Arts Decoratifs et Industriels Modernes in Paris in 1925. If not act one, scene one, the fair was nevertheless an early instance of the shock of this particular new. Critical response was divided, as it inevitably is. But not for the Americans, who were no-shows at the international event. In early 1926, *House & Garden* weighed in with a diatribe by Frank Alvah Parsons. Parsons, who went on to become president of Parsons School of Design, the academy founded by

In 1999, Pieter Estersohn photographed the exotic space that designer Muriel Brandolini created from a blah Manhattan bachelor pad. Brandolini established the interior drama at the foyer: she upholstered the wall in an arresting linen-and-velvet wallcovering, covered the floor with a vibrant tribal rug, and installed a Chinese red-lacquered table.

William Merritt Chase in 1896 (which trained, among others, Edward Hopper, Jasper Johns, and Norman Rockwell), is today remembered for instituting a curriculum designed to improve the quality, beauty, and function of mass-produced things. About the designs of Ruhlmann, Sue et Mare, Andre Gouli, and others, Parsons wrote: "Here a chair looks like a hunchback. There a table has dropsical legs. Yonder bed is suffering from elephantiasis...It seems a pity that in France of all countries should appear this strange and macabre manifestation. We have watched it growing in Vienna, in Moscow, and in Munich, but when it captured Paris last summer...we wondered if France, after all, had won the war. It would almost seem that in the household arts she had capitulated to the countries east of the Rhine. Verdun did not let them pass, but they managed to creep in under the shadow of the home."

The war of words has been waged on many fronts, and sometimes on front pages, as the clash of titans from the Beaux Arts and the Bauhaus has played itself out in houses and interiors across America—and around the world. After the Second World War, with Europe in need of rebuilding, and America poised for a massive construction and population boom, the pendulum swung—toward Modernism, in matters domestic as in everything else. Parsons, obviously, had prevailed. In part, the stripped-down, opened-up, free-flowing point of view that came to characterize so many houses and interiors in mid- and late-twentieth-century America may have reflected larger cultural issues. It also may have stemmed from the fact that many of Europe's great modern architects and designers had emigrated to the States in the late 1930s and early 1940s. These were the people who would not only build much of America during the second half of the century but who also trained the next generation of America's designers—the ones who would go on first to abjure the history of ornament and the decorative arts, and then to find some kind of difficult postmodern compromise with it.

Americans have always had a theatrical bent, as well as a taste for domestic plots both high and low. Perhaps it descends from the revolutionary spirit. When it comes to interior drama, though, there are as many traditions as there are Americans. We immigrate, and we decorate, and we assimilate—or not, as the case may be. We know that freedom of expression is every American's constitutional right. And while it may have taken us the better part of a century to acquire the confidence, and the technology, to turn our houses into home theaters, now, as always, we open them to public view—and thrill to the audience response.

In 2001, François Halard photographed the Villa Foscari, also know as La Malcontenta, for a magazine feature called "The Most Beautiful House in the World." The villa, just outside Venice, which was built around 1560 by Andrea Palladio, is filled with frescoes based on Ovid's *Metamorphoses*. The house has changed hands many times over the centuries but was reacquired in the early 1970s by architect and historian Antonio Foscari, a descendant of the original owner, and his wife, architect Barbara Del Vicario. The master bedroom has frescoes with a garden motif, the headboard of the bed is covered in strips of sixteenth-century fabric. As Del Vicario says, "One never gets used to beauty. One keeps being surprised and inspired by it."

Above: Philip C. Johnson designed the dining room of Mr. and Mrs. A. M. Burden's apartment (he was the president of New York's Museum of Modern Art at the time) to show off the art—such as the large Matta on the wall—and to showcase "their taste for good modern design." The window wall is hung with alternating panels of Siamese silk; their colors subdued by a gauze overcurtain. Photographed in 1954 by Pedro Guerrero, the room also includes a suspended ceiling grid made of brass tubes that contain pinpoint spots.

Right: "More than the menu, decoration keys the mood of any meal," the magazine proclaimed. The dining room of Helena Rubinstein (who was calling herself Princess Gourielli at the time) is a dream, with creamy walls and Salvador Dalí's three-part mural of morning, noon, and night (alas, only part of the surrealist trinity is visible here). If, as the article "Designed for Dining" stated, décor starts a "good flow of conversation," Rubinstein's guests must have had a gabfest analyzing Dali and reflecting on their hostess's collection of blue American glass. While few readers could afford these accoutrements, surely Haanel Cassidy's 1948 photograph was food for thought, inspiring them to dramatize their own dining rooms and to worry less over what to serve at mealtime.

Pages 14-15: In a 1950 feature called "How Creative People Use Color," the magazine stated, "Color is the personal equation in your life. What colors you respond to instinctively, how and where you use them (and in what amounts in any given room), is the key to your personality." Among the rooms used to illustrate this theory was the bedroom that couturier Marcel Rochas designed for his wife and himself. In 1954 André Kertész photographed the room, which features wall murals in the style of the eighteenth century, a high ceiling painted light blue, and a bed draped in icy blue-white satin.

Above: Walter Dorwin Teague, once considered the dean of industrial design, put together this executive lounge, photographed by Robert M. Damora in 1939, for the Ford Pavilion at the New York World's Fair. As the accompanying article, "Trends of Tomorrow," noted, "Among the executive suites, that designed by Walter Dorwin Teague for the Ford Exposition is perhaps most significant. It is an example of Modern in its purer phases and at its most elegant."

Right: "What is extraordinary about Mr. and Mrs. Frederick Mann's apartment in Philadelphia," wrote the magazine's editors in 1953, "is how well it adapts to their way of living. Everywhere is evidence of the two consuming loves that Mr. and Mrs. Mann share with their four growing daughters: music and hospitality." It seems a little odd that their love of art isn't mentioned, since they had a Modigliani hanging in their dining room, photographed by William Grigsby.

Ezra Stoller © Esto

Pages 18-19: Set designer Marla Weinhoff composed this fantasy room, photographed by Raymond Meier, for a young female pop star, vintage 2001. Weinhoff brought in pop and op art to give the space some intellectual heft. As she said, if the young singers of today "thought as much about their interiors as their wardrobe," they might land in a room like this one. "It's kind of a wish list," she noted, "the sensibility those girls should have."

Above: Paul Rudolph rode the swell of mid-century modernism to create some of this country's most distinctive and captivating houses and interiors. In the Deering residence in Casey Key, Florida, photographed by Ezra Stoller in 1960, Rudolph designed a two-story loggia overlooking the beach. The double glass doors in the corner open to the exterior. Five steps lead to the living room, on the second level, which can be closed off with sliding doors.

Left: For her home on the Cycladic island of Santorini, architect Lilia Melissa reinvented a ruined eighteenth-century house from the ground up. Blending the pragmatism of twentieth-century design with the captivating geometries and the colors of the wall paintings in Bronze Age houses uncovered at Santorini's great archaeological sites, Melissa created a dramatic residence that suits both herself and the ancient island. Among the place's most mysterious elements is the interior stair, photographed in 2000 by William Abranowicz.

Above: This relatively simple boudoir in the Elwood Whitneys' New York apartment is filled with grace notes. Emelie Danielson's photograph from 1939 captures the sense of uncrowded space, which is embellished with a Venetian mirror, a seahorse-and-shell chair in front of the vanity, and a window framed in net ruching.

Right: Interiors often benefit from the principle what goes around comes around. In this case, the charming guest bedroom features *faux bois* inspired by those that Christian Bérard made for a room at the Institut Guerlain designed by Jean Michel Frank in 1939. The whole of this Upper East Side town house, photographed in 2000 by Pieter Estersohn, was done in moderne style by decorator John Barman with his associate Jack Levy. Some of the house's contents are originals, including the Dorothy Draper table, which dates to the 1940s. Other pieces are reproductions.

There are more ways to give life and glamour to "mere walls," the magazine noted in 1933, than by repainting or papering them. Decorator Joseph Mullen made a disarmingly simple arrangement of swooping ropes and carved wood tassels on a dove gray bedroom wall. In a charming but slightly offbeat touch, a pair of porcelain hands seem to pop through the wall to catch up the ropes above the bed. A photo studio called The 3 recorded both the romantic shadow play and geometric order in the room. In the midst of the Depression, this eye-catching but inexpensive method of making a space luxurious must have been welcome.

Above: This elegant bedroom is a red sea of sumptuous fabrics. Silks, perhaps, or satins sweep down to the bed and swaddle it; they cushion the chairs and cling to the woman seated there. In fact, the material highlighted in Horst P. Horst's luscious 1949 photograph is cotton. The article "Cottons: Better Behaved Than Ever" describes the latest in finishing processes, printing methods, and dyes that were transforming the simple material. As Horst made evident, cotton had become as rich as could be.

Pages 26-27: Sometimes love is in the air, as it was for the person who bought this sixteenth-century palazzo in Venice and restored it to its previous frescoed glory. The owner wanted the hall, which overlooks the Grand Canal, to have the feeling of a ballroom, so she left it quite spare—an Italian Empire chaise, Flemish tapestries, and two eighteenth-century wrought-iron candelabra. "If romance is the leitmotif of this palace," wrote Marella Caracciolo, "the dramatic decorations pay tribute to it," as does Nadir's 1997 photograph.

In the late twentieth century, the aesthetic pendulum swung back toward the rigorous, stripped-down elegance characteristic of modernism's first wave more than 50 years earlier. This spare, light-filled interior by Michael Gabellini incorporates some contemporary design classics, such as the sofa and the reproductions of Yoshio-Tanaguchi's chairs for Tokyo's Hotel Okura. A photograph of Marcel Duchamp by Man Ray hangs over the sofa. Todd Eberle's 1998 photograph suggests Gabellini's credo: "I try to create a space with an emotional center."

Above: When in Manhattan, playwright Eugene O'Neill and his wife, Carlotta Monterey, lived in a duplex filled with mementos of their travels. The stairwell, which was photographed by Anton Bruehl in 1932, was painted green and "ornamented with a collection of macabre African masks and rare native drums that Mr. O'Neill brought home from French equatorial Africa."

Left: In a 1966 article titled "Fresh Swingy Ideas from Rooms of Young Pros," editors suggested that young decorators are naturally more adventurous than older ones: "The young pros use paint and wallpaper, for instance, in fresh, unconventional ways." Among the ideas to consider was that of combining casual, modest things with a few fine furnishings. Decorator Leoda de Mar's own residence, with wallpaper on the ceiling, photographed in 1966 by William Grigsby, provided one such example.

For a New York loft occupied by the publisher of a New York newspaper, his wife, and their two extremely active sons, designer Michael Formica created an open, modern space filled with humorous elements. Melanie Acevedo captured some of its delightful quirks on film in 2000, such as this place in the study where the woman in the Michael Gentile painting seems to be watching the jury-rigged chest of drawers (by Tejo Remy for the avant-garde Dutch design firm Droog) in the moment of collapse.

In the 1960s, Americans developed a taste for pavilion living. This version, photographed by William Grigsby in 1964, is more or less permanent. Constructed of acrylic panels set in a wood frame and capped with a plastic domed skylight, the six-sided structure "might alternate as the focus of summer parties and a private retreat," the magazine's editors suggested.

Above: In the 1950s, Palm Springs was a modernist's paradise. No one put more of a stamp on the place than the adventurous architect Albert Frey, whose firm, Clark & Frey, designed this inside grotto for the master himself. Photographed in 1950 by Julius Shulman, Frey's solarium pool invades a corner of his living room, creating the impression of a permeable boundary between interior and exterior. Sliding glass walls add to the effect, as do the plantings of banana, jasmine, ginger, and bamboo.

Right: Cecil Beaton was among the masters of the calculated dramatic effect in photography as well as in dress, set, and costume designs (remember, he won an Oscar for his work on *My Fair Lady*). In 1950, he had just finished work on this two-bedroom apartment in New York's Sherry Netherland Hotel. The duplex, photographed by André Kertész, is filled with strong and clashing colors, such as scarlet flocked wallpaper and regal blue upholstery, that are counterbalanced by graphic displays of black and white.

Above: Katharine Brush, best-selling author of *Red-Headed Woman* and *Young Man of Manhattan*, appears to have been an early modernist, at least as far as décor. Her combination studio/library, photographed in 1934 by F. S. Lincoln, featured walls lined in redwood burl with German silver moldings and a black-welted green leather wainscot. The chairs were black satin trimmed with green cord. The redwood burl desk with green leather top sat atop a green and black carpet. The space was conceived by Joseph Urban, the emigré Austrian architect known for his designs for Florence Ziegfeld (both the theater and the sets for the Follies), the New School for Social Research, and the Hearst Magazine Building.

Right: House owners in suburban St. Louis gave architect-designer Samuel Marx carte blanche in their spacious new residence, photographed in 1945 by the Hedrich-Blessing Studio. The staircase, which resembles the interior of an oversized shell, swirls upward, its curves in vivid contrast to the sharp lines of the windows and chair below.

There's something arresting and luxurious about all-white spaces, especially in urban interiors, where white has a tendency not to stay white for long. But designer Jennifer Post wields white with considerable discipline and to great effect, as this New York apartment photographed by Antoine Bootz in 2001 attests. Obviously flexible, functional, and bright, this monochromatic dining room seems full of life, and even, somehow, of color.

Pride of Place

It is a truth universally acknowledged that there's no place like home. That, of course, is where both our pride and our prejudices lie. Home means different things to different people. How you define it, and where, and when, you find it, can be the work of a lifetime, or it can arrive (on a good day) with three clicks of the heels. Home, after all, is the sense of self—expressed in tangible terms. The nature of that expression may change over time, as experiences accrue through emotional odysseys or physical ones. But the homing instinct, like the sense of self, is essentially an exultation of place. It asserts itself equally, although differently, at various stops along life's way. The pride we take in decorating and redecorating our own rooms, whether they're childhood bedrooms or first apartments, first houses or empty nests, remains the same, even when the places don't.

From the start, American magazines of all types have understood that the American character is the product of family and friends, and also of surroundings. In admitting that our environments can shape us to a greater or lesser degree, we also acknowledge that the house itself matters—not in the abstract, and not just as a system of walls and roofs designed to protect and defend its occupants from harsh elements or hostile neighbors. Civilization, after all, is acquired through civilizing influences, the design of the home among them. Shelter magazines have always addressed that fact of American life quite directly. Those that have documented the American home during the past century have chronicled, from the inside, a peculiarly American journey from doubt to certainty, from isolation to engagement, from conformity to idiosyncrasy, from periphery to center.

Americans have always been given to invention and expansion, of our selves and of our homes. We have a collective passion for improvement that is, really, just another manifestation of the promise of opportunity inherent in the American dream. Yet, as individuals, we can still find ourselves vulnerable to the gaze of others, embarrassed by unshed provincialisms, eager to discover and surround ourselves with the better thing for the sake of later transformation. Whether that happens to be an older, more sophisticated, more gracious style of living than our cousins across the oceans espouse, or something determinedly down-home and as American as apple pie

When Lord Snowdon took this photograph in 1998, Sister Parish had long been the acknowledged doyenne of American decorating—a role she filled with great panache. Arbiter of taste for the Astors, Rockefellers, Gettys, and Whitneys, decorator of choice for the Oval Office during the Kennedy years, Sister Parish defined the American ideal of luxurious comfort for the second half of the twentieth century.

or an Amish quilt, it hardly matters—we can try it on for size, and, if we find it suits us, keep it until we find ourselves ready for something else.

At the turn of the twentieth century, as we headed into the so-called century of progress, America as we now know it had yet to be built. Americans were deeply concerned with making decisions that were both good and right, and that might result in communities that would make manifest the ambitions of our optimistic youth, the certainties of our expanding place in the world, and the deepening pleasures of our growing wealth and confidence at home. American magazines began this campaign by finding and documenting the best models for their readers to copy—imitation being a necessary step on the path to identity, as well as the sincerest form of flattery.

In addition to recording changing styles and attitudes about living, magazines about house and home have also tended to serve as something of a looking glass, reflecting the shifting undercurrents of larger questions of identity and society. It's interesting to note that, through the years in *House & Garden*, photographs of people in their homes reveal that women seem to welcome readers in, even dressing to complement the décor. Men, in contrast, often seem to stand their ground. They may welcome visitors, but their body language says, "This is my turf. I'm here to protect it."

Perhaps it's true, as the great lyricist Johnny Mercer wrote in 1946, that "anyplace I hang my hat is home." But, as Stephen Sondheim asked twenty-four years later, "does anyone still wear a hat?" Customs change. The house that is celebrated one year as an architectural masterpiece may be vilified the next. What matters is that we feel at home where we live, that we make our own mark there, that we cut the cloth of domestic fashion to fit ourselves, not someone else's notion of us. In America, people tend to prize their homestead above all, whether it's a rambling estate out West, or a cozy apartment on Manhattan's West Side. "This is me," our residences say. "This is what, and who, I am."

Jason Schmidt snapped skateboarding legend Tony Hawk in 2002 while executing one of his signature moves, over the hood of a $45,000 handcrafted lilac-painted 1965 Bentley S3. If Hawk ever got his hands on an S3, and replaced the two Lexuses in his garage, he'd certainly make a few changes: "I'd definitely keep the radio and dash, but I'd hide an audio/video system inside the upholstery."

Pages 46-47: When actor Robert Montgomery moved his family west, they all wanted a house that looked like the colonial farm they had left behind in New York—so they built one in Beverly Hills. His wife, Elizabeth, wrote about the process and the finished result in a 1938 issue. About this photograph, taken by Fred Dapprich, she reported, "The favorite room in the Montgomery ménage is the library. It is filled with all the elements of comfort. Mr. Montgomery has settled into a giant couch (over ten feet long) designed especially at his request."

Above: Fashion designer Manuela Pavesi collects clothes. She's been doing this since the 1970s. And though she's not quite sure how many pieces she actually has, the collection itself occupies a large room where Paolo Barbi photographed her in 1999. In a case like Pavesi's, organization is all. She stores her finds in "genre-based" sections—one cupboard for embroidered Indian garments, and another for Victorian dresses. But the separation of powers only exists for clothes on the hanger. Pavesi loves "to mix early Chanel with new Prada. It's very crazy, but I try."

Right: What would a formal Renaissance garden be without the requisite classical statue? That, fortunately, is not a question that the Corsinis, who recently restored the family palazzo in Florence, need to ask. Statues may seem more populous there than humans, but there is still plenty of room for pets and people. The Corsini place demonstrates the family belief that "we should enjoy the beautiful things that have been passed down. That includes, as Michael T. McDermit's photograph from 2000 shows, everything from statuary to old plans, trunks, and other remnants of history.

Above: For Peter Joseph and Wendy Evans Joseph, and their children, furniture isn't just furniture—it's art. The two filled their Long Island house with the pieces they've collected by Wendell Castle, John Dunnigan, and Edward Zucca, among others. In this 1998 photograph by François Dischinger, their son demonstrates how the family experiences art as a way of life at home. The chair is by Mario Bellini, the desk by Gaetano Pesce, the rug by Gerhard Richter, the lamp by Albert Paley, and the screen by Wharton Esherick.

Right: In the 1960s, Palm Springs was an inviting landscape for enthusiasts of modernism, among them Albert Frey. In 1996, Frey was photographed by Dewey Nicks in the 1,200-square-foot house with an exposed steel frame and corrugated metal roof that Frey built for himself in 1964. The then 93-year-old Swiss-born architect, once the sorcerer Le Corbusier's apprentice, had lived in the California desert Eden since 1934. A lifetime of yoga made Frey flexible, a good thing for someone who made a career of standing accepted truths about design on their head.

Hello, Dolly. In 1965, Carol Channing was photographed by John Rawlings back where she belongs, which was at home, in an apartment in New York's Waldorf Towers, with her son, Channing. The magazine noted that the place where the actress lived her off-stage life as the wife of TV writer-producer Charles Lowe was "bursting with color and brimming over with books, drawings, and a lifetime's photographs."

One absolutely ought to take pride of place in one's own home, as Eartha Kitt does here. Photographed in 1999 by François Dischinger, the purring chanteuse drapes herself over a sofa that sits in front of a wall filled with portraits—of herself. And why not?

Above: Hedrich-Blessing Studio's 1947 image of a man washing a vast expanse of glass illustrates the promise of "bigger windows for less work." But there's a subtext: the larger the window, the better the view for those inside, and, equally important, the more those outside—the Joneses— can see of the mid-century affluence within. Matched sofas gird the coffee table; ashtrays and magazines are leisure-time artifacts of a new era of prosperity and uniformity.

Left: After five years of gardening for himself at Highgrove, the Prince of Wales traded up to large-scale farming by establishing the Duchy Home Farm on his estate's 1,085 acres. Prince Charles hired David Wilson, an agricultural school graduate photographed by Melanie Acevedo in 2000, to manage the farm's conversion to fully organic production. The profits from the produce go to the Prince of Wales Charitable Foundation.

Above: No one could accuse architect Philip Johnson of going to the dogs, except in the case of the house he designed for his two keeshond pups in 1999. Photographed by Todd Eberle with Alice (James was camera shy) in his arms, Johnson refers to the fan-shaped structure as an "ossuary" because the two canines like to store bones inside it. The term, said writer Susan Morrison, "is peculiarly apt, since the doghouse is also a half-inch scale model for a grave marker that Johnson conceived for a client's future use. But for now," she added, "it stands, like the nearby Glass House, as another of the remarkable living spaces produced by a remarkable man."

Right: Collectors are born, not made. In order to stave off curio chaos, some strict discipline is required, as Simon Doonan and Jonathan Adler demonstrate. The two have eclectic tastes, so they use a carefully chosen color palette to create a highly personal sort of order. Photographed by Todd Eberle at home in 1997, Doonan, standing, and Adler pose at a George Nelson table filled with the pottery Adler makes. The dog, a guest, sits happily in a Saarinen chair.

Deep in the heart of Montmartre, furniture designer Hubert Le Gall saws, melts, and sculpts his charming designs, which include the oversized velvet flowerpot that divides to become two Empire club chairs. Le Gall calls his designs "fantasy objects," and he makes them because "it amuses me. Otherwise life is boring." In this 2002 photo by Alexandre Bailhache, it's clear that Le Gall's designs amuse others as well as himself—in this case, his two nieces, Annabel and Iris.

Above: Not too many celebrities today would pose for a magazine feature titled "How the Stars Entertain Themselves" by looking down the barrel of a gun. But Gary Cooper, photographed by Coburn in 1942, was a screen hero minted by Hollywood and scripted by Hemingway (remember *Farewell to Arms* and *For Whom the Bell Tolls*?). He was expected to have a knotty–pine huntin' and fishin' room with a well-stocked gun case and taxidermic evidence that he could live hard, dress well, and still shoot straight.

Right: Couturiers should always dress for the occasion. Carolina Herrera shows us how by donning formal wear for a photo essay on moving day. She was photographed in 1997 by Claus Wickrath as she and her husband were decorating their new home and hanging the wonderful collection of paintings he inherited from his mother. "Moving is hell," Herrera said. "Packing up, you uncover things you forgot about years ago. Unfortunately, we didn't find any diamonds."

Pages 64-65: Chris Sander's 1998 photograph gives another meaning to the term "window seat." Michael Simon, an interior designer with a passion for eighteenth-century furniture, was caught on film eyeing the superb François Reuze sofa he had purchased at Sotheby's. The sublime seat was so big that it had to be hoisted into his New York apartment. After noting that the sofa was just as beautiful from underneath as it was from the usual vantage point, Simon said, "I'm the only thing in this place that isn't from the eighteenth century, and all of it will outlive me."

Right: David Seidner took this portrait of Marie-Chantal of Greece, née Miller, in 1998. At the time, the Princess and her husband, Pavlos, the Prince, were putting together their just-bought Connecticut home. They decorated the Greenwich house with a mixture of wedding presents and family heirlooms, as well as notable art and objects. The spirit of the house, like that of its owner, is youthful, but without frivolity.

Pages 68-69: Artists make spaces their own in many different ways, as François Halard's 1996 photograph of painter Judith Hudson and writer Richard Price's Greenwich Village living room reveals. Rough plaster and traces of dripping paint on the walls echo Hudson's style on canvas. Patterned kilims and embroidered and embellished textiles bring the touch of the hand and the wide and various world into this city residence. Then there's skateboarder Genevieve Hudson-Price, who sprawls across the sofa in the way one can only at home.

Pages 70-71: Design may be a dog's life, suggested a series of 1998 photographs by William Wegman, but it's definitely here to sit and to stay. In this photo, the Wegman weimaraners cozy up on the sectional seating. Perhaps this sofa is a conversation stopper for four-legged friends, but it's definitely a conversation piece for the two-legged variety, who should do plenty of chin-wagging on it—and about it.

Right: From a spectacular perch in a favorite maple tree in northwestern Connecticut, the late fashion designer and New York Public Library trustee Bill Blass went on the record about his passion for reading: "Reading is a way of being alone in a wide world of escape. It means I'm never bored." Blass, who was photographed here by Pascal Chevallier in 1997, went on to explain that, contrary to rumors, he wasn't writing a book, although he did have that idea in mind. "And no," he concluded, "there isn't a fictional character I try to copy. After all, I invented myself."

Domestic Bliss

The organization man is one thing; the organized person, quite another. But all housework with no time to play house makes even the most organized person dull. Americans have long invested in an idea of modernity which says that convenience leads to bliss. This has turned us into happy consumers, particularly of gadgets and gizmos that make life easier by saving time and reducing effort. From their earliest days, shelter magazines have endeavored to help their readers run their houses smoothly, and thus their lives. Born not all that long after the incandescent lightbulb (which Edison perfected in 1882, the same year he opened the first commercial power station in New York City), or the petrol-powered automobile, and just a year after Thorstein Veblen's *Theory of the Leisure Class* appeared, American publications devoted to houses and gardens have documented an American century driven by the tension between machine-age innovation and its backlash, the rage against the machine.

As dialectics go, that of change versus constancy may be trite—but it's true. Creating the time for leisure by decreasing the difficulty and tediousness of housework has long been a goal of American housewives. It still is, even after a century's worth of need and consumption has generated and made obsolete a host of things designed to meet that goal.

The surprise is just what a flood of gadgets there have been, and how long we have had them. In 1907, C. D. Wood, an operative of the New York Edison Company, advised *House & Garden* readers, "Whether the mistress of an establishment 'does her own work' or has a retinue of servants to do it for her, she is more comfortable and better served if her home is equipped with those electrical appliances which lighten all domestic labor." Among the appliances Wood listed were electric stoves, refrigerators, washers and dryers, irons, plate warmers, knife sharpeners, coffee grinders, meat choppers, dishwashers, potato peelers, fans, toasters, coffee percolators, radiators, water heaters, curling irons, chafing dishes, shoe polishers, cereal cookers, egg boilers, sewing machines, and cigar lighters—first-generation versions of the same mod cons that we cherish at home today.

Fashion designer and stylist Ann Shore arranged her London house in a series of vivid, charming, personal tableaux. She is an assembler of objects and images, and delights in the art of arrangement. When Melanie Acevedo photographed Shore's kitchen in 2000, the refrigerator and the adjacent wall were covered with photos and postcards. "I covered it with a collage of black-and-white images," said Shore, "instead of having it sit there as a big white blob."

In the twentieth century, the machine as machine has never been enough. It must also have soul, of a sort, or it won't be worth its weight in the future, for which, of course, it's not designed. As an existential conundrum, it's a poser of the first order—especially as manifested in the home. Certainly, finding the sublime in the man-made was a force behind the modern movement in architecture and design. What else can Le Corbusier possibly have meant when he wrote in *Towards a New Architecture*, his 1923 manifesto, "A house is a machine for living in. Baths, sun, hot water, cold water, warmth at will, conservation of food, hygiene, beauty in the sense of good proportion"?

Status has always been one of the driving forces behind the culture of consumption—even when the consumption is of less, not more. But let's not forget that gadgets—indeed, the entire history of invention, as well as the notion of progress—exist at all because someone, somewhere, has figured out a way to reduce work, or to increase productivity, which, by any other name, means creating more work in the name of more free time. It's an equation that has never really balanced.

While very few people—other than, say, Dr. Skinner—want to live in machines, they do want to occupy houses that work like the proverbial well-oiled machine. And certainly few house owners could match those efficiency fiends Frank and Lillian Gilbreth, immortalized in the book *Cheaper by the Dozen*. Readers needed guidance, and as the twentieth century's cataclysmic events and scientific developments brought enormous social changes, the shelter magazines kept pace, acting as informers, advisers, and tour guides to the home front.

How do you run a house with servants—or, more to the point, without them? What is that weird material the architect wants to use in the addition to the house? What about that gizmo in the kitchen? Families may have gotten smaller over the decades, but houses have gotten bigger, and full of more things that need attention: washing, painting, touching up, wiring. We need to arrange them well, to store them intelligently and handsomely. Now that we can tackle the most mundane household tasks with deliberate ease, we can savor the benefits of the well-run house and realize that efficiency is both an art and a science—and that leisure is domestic bliss.

As the century progressed, readers began to appreciate and feel comfortable with new technology and new materials. A 1948 issue focusing on "servantless living" assured consumers that graciousness did not depart with the maid and the cook. Herbert Matter took this striking photograph of a dishwasher, just one household appliance that, as *House & Garden* put it, "works tirelessly and competently, takes no time off, and never answers back."

Above: This heady still life by Anton Bruehl accompanied the 1937 article "Electrical Gadgets Serve You with Efficiency," which celebrated the latest in appliances. In the modern house, Bruehl's photograph tells us, everything is shining and useful.

Right: Industrial designers spent the twentieth century making modern conveniences in snazzy packages to tempt fashion-conscious consumers. The twenty-first century promises to be no different, as this sexy little juicer, photographed by Carlton Davis in 2001, demonstrates.

Pages 80-81: The American sense of bliss comes from the fact that as a country we have been able to produce far more food than we can consume. During the Second World War, Americans cultivated their Victory Gardens to feed themselves and the troops overseas. The caption to this 1948 photograph by Horst P. Horst stated the equation of our comfort, "'Food = Freedom' What you raise this year will make possible larger food shipments abroad, help to free the starving from fear, help to free ourselves from the pricks of our own conscience."

Above: The most recent expression of America's passion for permutation is the recycling fever that swept the country in the late 1990s with the realization that greenhouse gases and global warming were going to affect our comfortable futures. Jay Zukerkorn's 1998 photograph of bottles in the iconographic blue recycling bag symbolizes the recycling aesthetic that was, according to editors, "having an impact on the design of kitchens, lamps, birdhouses, and vases."

Right: When fashion journalist Holly Brubach moved to Milan, she changed many things about her life—but not one of the most important ones. A self-confessed fitness addict, Brubach works out regularly—bodybuilding, not aerobics. Rehydration is a necessity in her case, not a luxury. But, as Michael Wooley documented in 1999, a refrigerator filled with bottled water is more than mere domestic bliss: it's a photo opportunity.

By the late 1930s, Frank Lloyd Wright had developed the carport, which solved the problem of how to integrate the function of the garage into the form of the house. The idea of the overhang was picked up by the modern architects of the mid-century, including Marcel Breuer, who designed this house on Long Island with a second story that cantilevers over the first—thereby creating parking space right outside the front door. Ezra Stoller's photograph demonstrates that at home, as elsewhere, convenience really is bliss. Breuer's 1947 house has a compact frame and an open-plan interior that demonstrate the prevailing trend toward a more informal, servantless lifestyle. And, as the magazine noted, "in the cantilevered house you get more living space out of your building dollar."

Page 86: For many people, life is a bowl of cherries. But for *House & Garden*'s cooking editor, June Platt, strawberries were equally fruitful. Samuel Gottscho photographed Platt in 1939 while she was hulling berries prior to putting up some jam. According to the accompanying article, she and her husband had just purchased this old New Jersey farmhouse as an anodyne to their hectic city existence.

Page 87: There are lots of dirty secrets in the world of domestic bliss. One of them is that, for some, household chores such as vacuuming are truly pleasures—even restorative forms of escape. Take, for example, "The Art of Sucking Up," a piece on hoovering that ran in a 1996 issue. Even celebrities do it, as this Max Vadukul photograph of a pj-wearing Isaac Mizrahi with his vacuum cleaner documents. Mizrahi admits, "With my Virgo ascendant, laundry and vacuuming are some of my favorite activities. Of the two, vacuuming a room that really needs it is my favorite. More of a purge than anything."

Left: They call it puppy love, and for good reason. There may be nothing more endearing than letting a sleeping dog lie next to a favorite chartreuse suede sling-back, as Christopher Craymer's 2001 photograph demonstrates.

The mother and
child reunion,
wrote Paul Simon,
is only a moment
away. It's a
moment that has
animated much of
the history of art.
And certainly it's a
domestic moment
to be treasured,
as Michel
Arnaud's 1996
photograph of
Marie Gersh
with her son Noah
cuddling on the
living room
sofa reveals.

91

Above: 'Tis the season to be jolly. A Philippe Starck gnome table can make even a curmudgeon giggle. At Christmas, as Victor Schrager's 2001 photo demonstrates, too much is never enough.

Right: Nothing freshens up a space more quickly than a new coat of pain. And there are many more hues than meet the eye. This 2003 photograph by Francesco Mosta reveals the joy of the mix as well as the difficulty of the match and the infinite power of white.

Pages 94-95: Splendor in the grass takes on a different meaning when the grass is part of a Renaissance garden that has been in the family since the seventeenth century. This Florentine garden continues to be a playground for a family who, as Michael T. McDermit's photograph from 2000 shows, still frolics and entertains among box hedges, ancient statues, and citrus trees.

Above: The riddle of the sphinx goes something like this: what has four legs in the morning, two legs at noon, and three legs at night? The answer, of course, is man. Humans tend to use the arrival of the next generation as an antidote to the inevitable close of this one. The same impulse urges us to acquire objects, and to invest them with our memories—and our hopes. Personal style is such that a collection and arrangement of objects in an interior can reflect the nature of an individual as well as the elemental facts of human existence. This 1998 photograph by Pieter Estersohn captures what Jacopo Etro, who lives in this apartment and is the uncle of the Buddha-like baby, says is the essential element of style: "Mixing the past with the future gives you a sense of timelessness."

Right: The baby boom, the economy, and technological development were in full swing, and all conspired to bring the arts home. Richard Rutledge's familial image from 1955 reflects the enormous cultural change. Electronic keyboards, tape recorders, portable TVs, and phonographs delivered music, dance, theater, and films as never before. Dad is, presumably, still at the office.

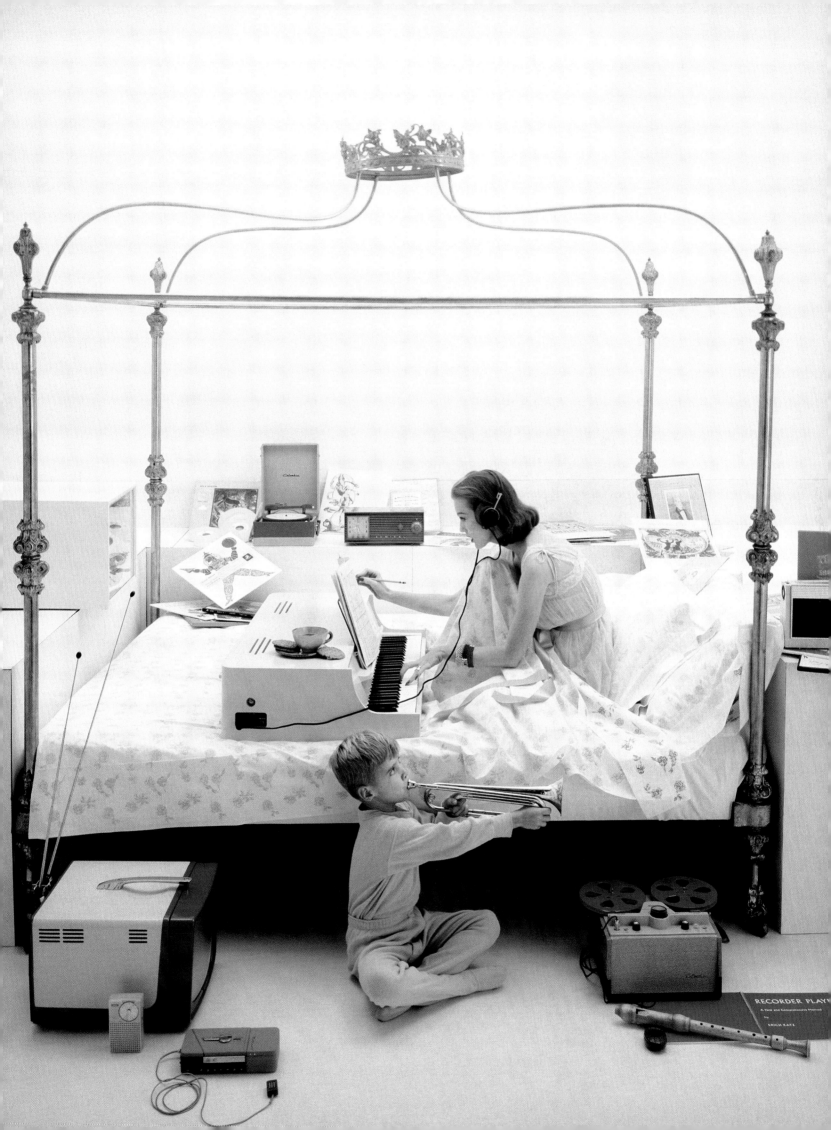

Above: Better living through chemistry extended to the closet. Dana B. Merrill's 1938 photograph introduced readers to the newly invented plastic Lucite, which transformed the humble clothes hanger into an up-to-the-minute accessory. Its transparency gave the hangers a modish lightness and sleekness that were perfect expressions of the time. The proud owner of this well-organized closet could have invited her friends to inspect a space that was as contemporary and fashionable as the clothes she kept there.

Right: Laundry is a necessity, but air drying (once the only way to go) is now a luxury—especially when clothes are hung on a line under the summer sun. Laundry rooms have been a concern of designers and homeowners for most of the twentieth century, as have the various appliances available to lighten the load of the wash-and-wear cycle. No doubt they always will be. Cleanliness and freshness never go out of style, not in 1998, when Eric Huang took this picture of lingerie and fine linens hanging in a light breeze, nor next year, nor probably in the next century.

When Tom Ford designed his first home collection for Gucci, he set his goals high. Ford wanted to create new classics that are obviously Gucci, but without any visible interlocking "Gs" or equestrian hardware. "My designs come from the house," he said. "I go through my own home, take old items, and change, stretch, and remake them." And so he has. Victor Schrager photographed Ford's silver and crystal pieces in 1997.

Garden Design

There is something democratic about dirt. Certainly, the roots of garden design in America go deep. We have been speeding the plough since the first settlers landed, cultivated an economy from the ground up, and loaded their tables with produce from kitchen gardens ringed with flowers. The founding fathers planted the seeds of American horticulture. Washington and Jefferson, gentlemen farmers both, tended acres at Mount Vernon and Monticello that continue to serve as useful models for the science and the art of garden design. Such ideas are meant for sharing, and were from the time of America's earliest magazines—one of which, *The Farmers Almanac*, first published by freeman Benjamin Banneker in 1792, could be considered the country's first magazine about house and garden.

American garden design is as much about nature as it is about nurture. Like the architecture of houses and the planning of cities, it has a long, complicated, rich tradition of grafting and cross-pollination. America's landscape tradition comes from England, and specifically from the scenic parks that Lancelot "Capability" Brown and Sir Humphry Repton devised in the eighteenth century for England's great country houses. Andrew Jackson Downing, a Repton disciple, pioneered America's green-space planning in the the mid-nineteenth century. A nursery owner and designer of country houses and gardens along the Hudson River, Downing wrote the urtext on American landscape design.

By the late-nineteenth century, Frederick Law Olmsted had staked out urban plans (and suburban ones) with verdant expanses. With Calvert Vaux, he designed many of the city parks and green spaces that remain among this country's most treasured, and visited. Olmsted, and his son Frederick, Jr., sketched plans for the nascent National Park system, which emphasized the need to preserve patches of the American Eden. Instrumental in founding the National Park Service and *The Nation* magazine, he also worked on private gardens for estates such as Biltmore.

To illustrate a 1976 interview with the remarkable myrmecologist (ant specialist) Edward O. Wilson, professor of zoology and curator of entomology at the Museum of Comparative Zoology, Harvard University, the magazine ran this Irving Penn photograph of a hand clutching dirt. Wilson had just published *Sociobiology*, a book that set the scientific world awhirl with its synthesis of biology, psychology, and anthropology. "If we can gain a sense of emotional reward from contemplating our environment and living closer to it," said Wilson, "perhaps our descendants might evolve further in that direction and discover deeper emotional rewards."

America's estate-planning phase lasted into the 1930s, and its garden tradition broadened to the cultivating cultures of France and Italy—and of Japan, China, Persia, and the Mediterranean countries. Enormous houses, surrounded by parks and formal gardens, bloomed across the country—as did the new profession of landscape architect. Tending the beds at home had long been women's work, which may be why this emergent field accepted women. The first bouquet of lady landscapers included Ellen Shipman, Beatrix Ferrand (Edith Wharton's niece), and Marion Cruger Coffin (an MIT graduate)—all of whom designed gardens for the country's newly landed gentry. Some of those gardens, such as Dumbarton Oaks and Winterthur, are now American treasures.

Gardeners hunt and gather, then they plant and transplant. Some explore the planet's wilds in the name of science, searching for new species to bring home for nurturing under glass at America's botanical centers and arboreta. Others trace a path through a local swamp or forest, or a neighbor's backyard, in pursuit of wild trillium or a cutting of wisteria. Many of these adventurers document their discoveries in the popular press as well as in the academic, for gardeners are people of the book—who spend the fallow season reading and planning for the next.

Community gardens, too, have a prideful place in the tradition of American garden design. Citizens have long carved growing spaces out of the very fabric of the cities, instituting order and encouraging happy accident in unexpected places. The community will to garden has never been more evident than during the Victory Garden movement of the Second World War—when able-bodied American citizens were asked to do for their country by growing vegetables in public parks, school yards, baseball fields, vacant lots, and their own backyards across the country. American publications contributed to the national effort, in which more than 20 million Americans participated. *House & Garden* did its share, and also developed an official Victory Garden logo.

American gardeners start young—about the same time they learn about contrary Mary, her silver bells, and her cockleshells. Each generation develops its serious gardeners, and its Sunday ones. We grow with our gardens, and our gardens grow with us. The urge to garden, as Richard Wilbur's lyrics to the finale of Leonard Bernstein's *Candide* make so clear, is just another expression of the American desire for improvement: "We're neither pure nor wise nor good; we'll do the best we know. We'll build our house, and chop our wood, and make our garden grow." So consider the lilies, how they grow, because, as it says in Matthew, they really are more magnificent than anything made by man.

In 1956, Georges Braun photographed the colorful concrete garden that landscape architects Eckbo, Royston & Williams designed for the San Francisco home of Dr. and Mrs. A. B. Chinn. Pigmented cement takes the place of flowers, and stays bright through all seasons. Some of the areas are troweled smooth; others have a pebbled surface. The rectangular plant beds are integral to the design. As the editors noted, "This example of happy outdoor living space is based on meticulous planning, practical construction, imaginative use of color, and one of the simplest, most satisfactory types of terrace paving for gardens."

Pages 106-107: Water gardens have a long and celebrated history. This one, on a Long Island estate called Gracefield, was designed by architect L. Alger and photographed in 1933 by a studio called The 3. According to the editors, the design was influenced by the traditional gardens of Spain and Morocco. The caption noted, "The pool, with its broad coping and cobbled walk, is located at the base of a steep, tree-covered slope which sets off admirably the massed masonry, the water arch, and the groups of immense water lilies."

Right: California architect Thornton Ladd designed a home and series of stepped garden terraces for himself in Pasadena, which Ezra Stoller photographed in 1957. Shown is the so-called Mondrian garden, which has a rigorous abstract geometric design composed of beds of sand and succulents interspersed with boulders.

Pages 110-111: City people with a love for the great outdoors often ascend to tar beach, or, in the case of Wendy Evans Joseph and her husband, Peter, a rooftop garden 39 stories above Manhattan. Linda Pollak, an architect and Harvard professor, designed an open space that stands up to howling winds, scorching sun, and downpours (a subroof supports the slate, fountain, and plants). Photographed by François Dischinger in 1998, the space serves as a playground by day and an aerie for entertaining by night.

Right: Architect Peter Wilson planned his garden pavilion to mirror the elements of the house he designed for himself and his wife on Fire Island. The garden, said the architect, "is actually part of the house." Photographed by Norman McGrath in 1982, the place, wrote Martin Filler, summons a wide variety of associations for different people: "Not only are the gardens of Renaissance Italy evoked, but the lush mixtures of luxuriant flowers that spill from the wedge-shaped beds also seem much in the English country garden tradition of carefully tended wildness."

Who says modernism and nature can't mesh?
Carla De Benedetti produced evidence that clearly
shows how they can when she photographed
Milanese architect Gae Aulenti's redesign of the
gardens for the Marchese and Marchesa Pucci's villa
in Tuscany in 1971. Aulenti terraced the land with
a rigorous geometry that nevertheless conforms
perfectly to the contours of the surrounding landscape.
She even punctuated the terraces with potted
lemon trees, in a nod to local tradition.

Conductor William Christie is nothing if not a formalist, as the garden he designed for the front of his house in the French countryside makes apparent. This walled garden, where a stray leaf is as welcome as Wagner orchestration in a Bach cantata, features miniature boxwood surrounded by crushed brick. The walled space with eighteenth-century wooden gates was photographed by François Halard in 1997.

Pages 118-119: However much it may be about engaging the natural world, gardening is always in some sense about interfering with nature, too. What looks at first like an outrageously artificial landscape is not so different from the work of sixteenth-century French garden designers who wanted their parterres to resemble the texture and pattern of a fashionable brocade. Artist Tori Winkler Thomas met the natural disaster of boxwood blight around her Virginia home in 1984 by drenching the dying bushes with latex house paint in what she described as "worn-out hues." A neighbor's horse, brought in by photographer Jacques Dirand, underlines the meeting of nature, art, and artifice.

Right: A 1940 issue on Washington, D.C., included Carola Rust's photograph of the Erwin Laughlin house and garden, which were designed by John Russell Pope, the architect of Union Station, the Jefferson Memorial, and the National Gallery of Art, as well as numerous residences. The garden, which was clearly based on the French tradition, centered on an open gravel space planted with a copse of linden trees, like those on Paris side streets. Editors noted, "The house with its gardens is a notable example of Louis XV style in this country."

Forty-eight years ago, landscape architect Dan Kiley brought his visionary modernism to Columbus, Indiana, where it continues to flourish. Kiley's famous allée of honey locusts, photographed by Dana Gallagher in 1999, culminates at Henry Moore's *Draped Reclining Woman*. The trees run along the length of a house designed by Eero Saarinen and Kevin Roche for J. Irwin Miller, an industrialist whose passion for modernism turned to a unique form of patronage that transformed Columbus into an architectural mecca.

Le Noviciat, photographed in 1949 by André Kertész, was designed by Patrice Bonnet, chief architect in residence of the neighboring Chateau de Versailles, for Commandant Paul-Louis Weiller and redecorated after the war by Lady Mendl (Elsie de Wolfe). "The gardens," wrote the editors, "which cleverly adapt ideas from the neighboring Park of Versailles to an everyday scale, are notable for a small green amphitheater and eighteenth-century statues." The square terrace consists of pockets of turf alternating with slate pavers; the surrounding statuary is by Le Poussin.

Landscape architect Douglas Reed, photographed by Gregory Heisler in 1998, stands with his dachshund Pookie on the stepping-stone bridge of his firm's acclaimed Therapeutic Garden for Children in Wellesley, Massachusetts. The garden's organizing element is the narrow steel-sided rill that winds through it, articulating the site's topography and defining individual spaces, each devoted to a distinct emotional experience.

Outdoor Living

For a little taste of heaven, just walk out your back door. Whether the space you step into is a porch or a lawn, a tennis court or a garden, it is not an adjunct to home, but an integral part of it. The American backyard, in all its permutations, has always been portrayed as a haven of dappled light, the place where we can shed the stress of contemporary civilization. Some of us may snooze or read, but sooner or later we all get up from our lounge chairs to find our inner sportsman.

America's early advocates of outdoor living are a formidable bunch: Emerson, Thoreau, Whitman, Audubon, Muir, and Theodore Roosevelt, to name just a few. But life for most Americans requires proximity to the city. The metropolis, however oppressive, is the starting point of the American dream. It's a landing point and a proving ground. If you can make it there, it's a fact that you can make it anywhere—including the suburbs, which is where paradise is regained for most Americans.

Americans tend to think of the suburb as a peculiarly American invention, as a post-World War II phenomenon, and as a particularly American life choice. It's not, although certainly Americans have made the suburb the most inhabited type of community during the second half of the twentieth century.

Frederick Law Olmsted and Calvert Vaux began planning the green spaces of Riverside, Illinois, a *ville* more rural than urban, in 1868. Thirty or so years later, English city planner Ebenezer Howard published *Garden Cities of Tomorrow*, the influential text that planted the seeds of Letchworth, England's first "garden city," and that inspired America's New Town movement. Backyards and green spaces proliferated rapidly around the country: Sunnyside Gardens, Queens, for example, designed by Clarence Stein and Henry Wright and built in the mid-to-late 1920s, and Radburn, New Jersey, designed by Stein and Wright and begun in 1928, a harbinger of the New Deal's Greenbelt towns. There's Broadacre City, Frank Lloyd Wright's utopian vision of the 1930s, and Le Corbusier's hybridized high-rise plans for tomorrow's garden cities, such as Ville Contemporaine and the Plan Voisin. After the Second World War, as both the building and baby booms exploded, George Nelson proposed

The late Pietro Porcinai was the wild card of European landscape design. His transformation of an Italian Renaissance garden, photographed by Frenando Bengoechea in 1997, brimmed with wit, and involved creating a tropical shrine enclosed by a thick bamboo hedge and the installation of such exotics as lotus. But it's the four-poster bed that he designed and placed poolside that really gives the place its insouciance.

"Grass on Main Street," an urban plan meant to stop white flight by seeding downtowns with suburban amenities. Construction began on Levittown in 1947. The reconsideration of the American utopia continues at Seaside, Florida, the ideal urban village planned by Andres Duany and Elizabeth Plater-Zyberk and started in the early 1980s, a community that continues to grow today.

American optimism has always expressed itself through utopian ideals and the zeal for social reform. The turn-of-the-century City Beautiful movement was one such noble adventure. Led by Daniel Burnham—the Chicago architect and builder responsible for the shining "White City," a paragon of Beaux Arts order, at Chicago's Columbia Exposition of 1893—and others, the City Beautiful movement suggested that cityscapes beautified by parks, gardens, and broad boulevards would help relieve the social ills of urban life, inspiring civic loyalty and moral rectitude among the poor. And building in the Beaux Arts idiom, they felt, would raise American cities to cultural parity with their European counterparts. Progressives and reformers such as Jacob Riis pushed hard for better living conditions, more access to air and light, and, among other amenities, playgrounds for children in the nation's inner cities. America's shelter magazines, especially *House & Garden*, provided a forum for disseminating these ideas. They also dispensed practical advice on choosing gear for outdoor activities, as well as year-round management of gardens, pets, and children.

Early in the century, formality reigned, even in outdoor pursuits. But two wars, a national highway system, and miles of rails later, the leisure class was no longer a theory—nor were leisure pursuits available only to the few. We wanted, in fact were eager, to engage with our own personal patch of the great outdoors. Perhaps there would be no backyard without Robert Moses, and other forces of nature like him. And perhaps their plans and desires have led to America's national flower being a concrete cloverleaf, as Lewis Mumford suggested. But the idea of America's wide-open spaces, even those neatly fenced in between white picket railings or clipped boxwood hedges, continues to beckon. The green spaces of our individual utopias invite us to horse around, swim, play a game, build a tree house, rummage in the tool shed, dig, plant, weed, or prune—to explore, compete, experiment, discover, or to mow. It's our manifest destiny—to which we say, enthusiastically, bully.

Surf's up at this Santa Barbara beach house designed by architect Andy Neumann, who floated an elliptical atrium clerestory element over the central portion of the house to bring as much bright light as possible into the interior. Photographed in 1998 by Todd Eberle, the house incorporates a beachy palette of mahogany, limestone, redwood, and granite.

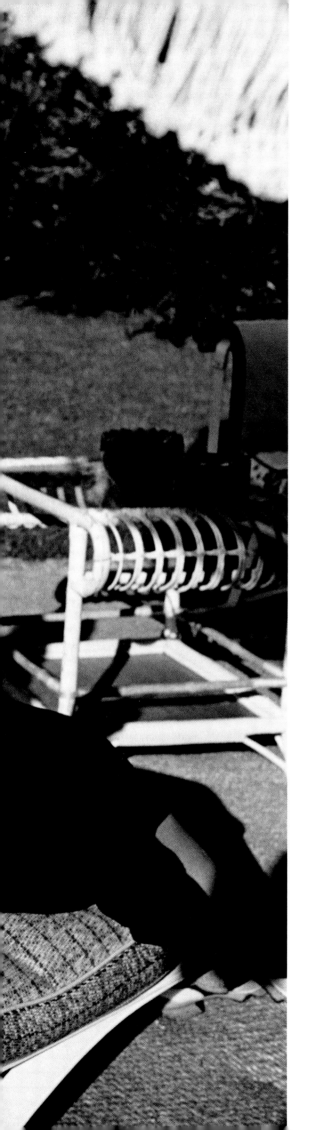

For a 1946 issue, editors went flying down to Rio, and Buenos Aires, and other points south where outdoor living is a natural extension of indoor life. Here, Luis Lemus captured Sra. Cora Kavanaugh lounging by the pool on the grounds that surround her French-inspired house, which was designed by an Argentinian architect by the name of Minvielle. Sra. Kavanaugh, stated editors, "numbers among her possessions the only skyscraper in Buenos Aires and an enviable collection of French antiques."

Outdoor play spaces for children generally consist of forts and tree houses constructed—usually in a haphazard kind of way—from materials scavenged around the neighborhood. There are more fantastic, Grimm-brothers-inspired options available, however, as this miniature Italianate villa makes clear. Photographed in 1998 by François Dischinger, the 8-foot by 10-foot by 11-foot house has a door that locks and windows that open. And, fitted with an adult-sized back door, it can be used as a toolshed or potting shed once its tenants have, like Alice, grown.

To accompany a 1948 article on tea by novelist Rumer Godden, photographer Tom Leonard recorded some American devotees of the tea ceremony. Here is Mrs. Robert Daniel, who, noted editors, pours tea every afternoon "beside a pool in one of the most romantic gardens in America, that of Brandon on the James in Tidewater, Virginia."

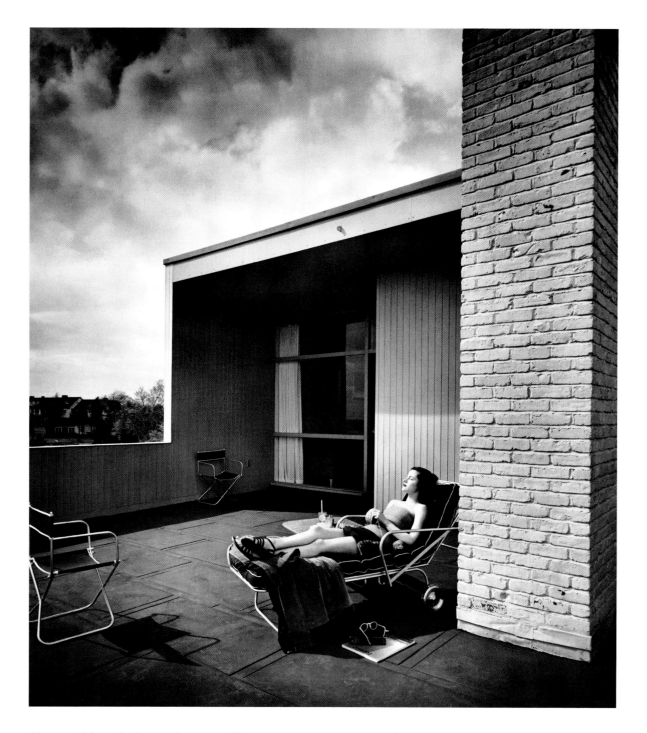

Above: Although the celebration of leisure time was a postwar luxury, it was one still best enjoyed in the solitude of a patio or roof terrace. After all, to really do nothing you need to be alone. In 1947, Ezra Stoller captured this sun worshiper whose knitting might well be a prop—a halfhearted concession to the world of purposeful pursuits.

Right: In 1937, photographer A. E. Boutrelle recorded the urban garden outside Mrs. Godfrey Goldmark's New York penthouse. The gardener used evergreens exclusively: plantings included mainly hemlocks, with golden cypress and golden arborvitae opposite all the windows.

Brigitte Lacombe
took this photograph
of the daughters of
Piero Sartogo and
Nathalie Grenon in
2000. The girls are
running through
a field of lavender
adjacent to the
family property near
Siena. The view from
the main house,
a Renaissance villa,
takes in a guesthouse
made from
the remains of
a medieval tower,
and a low
storage shed for
farm machinery.

A 1940 issue on the glories of "gay and casual" California living featured this photograph by Alexander Paal with the caption, "Playing is easy for Californians." There are two surprises here. To begin with, it is odd to find that such a splendid picture ran in a size only slightly larger than a postage stamp. But more than that, in a spirit of celebrity indifference, the magazine made nothing of the fact that the woman in the hoop was movie star Paulette Goddard. Gone are the days!

Above: While only the rich had tennis courts, everyone with a lawn could cash in on the craze for alfresco diversions like the English game of Miniten, beautifully photographed in 1937 by Alfred Eisenstaedt. Played with rackets called "thugs," made of two wooden disks, it looks like fun. And what happened to Miniten? It faded away along with other popular games of the times, such as lawn Hi-Li, Penguin Skittles, and Clown Quoits.

Pages 144-145: Seattle-based furniture designer Roy McMakin renovated the Berro residence in Los Angeles by restoring the 1907 Tudor façade and then adding a series of minimalist white boxes to create a pastiche that is part Stratford-on-Avon, part Le Corbusier, and definitely Hollywood. The white pool house, photographed in 2002 by Jason Schmidt, encloses the wry domestic tableau established by McMakin's furniture.

Magazine editors proposed the terrace kitchen in 1967, as this photograph by Pedro Guerrero documents. While everyone else in the family is living outdoors from sunup to midnight, asked the editors, why must the cook be cooped up in the kitchen? The answer, they said, is that she needn't be, as long as you can move the kitchen outdoors, too. This version features a stationary island with a mobile undercounter refrigerator and barbecue, among other amenities.

Pages 148-149: The photographer Hiro turned his camera on himself, more or less, when he took this picture of his palatial chicken coop in 1997. "It's really a birdhouse," he said of his Pennsylvania roost, "but my wife calls it a chicken mansion. When I was a boy in Peking, I used to keep chickens, and I'd make little houses for them. I'd go to sleep thinking about the fantasy birdhouses I wanted to build." Sixty years later, he made those dreams come true. "We bought some property, and I decided that for once I was going to build something from scratch." His silkies and Mille Fleur chickens clearly rule this roost. "They are very small and dainty. They look like a gang of angora sweaters," he says.

Right: The background of successful gardening, read the caption to this 1935 photo by Harold Haliday Costain, is work—honest work with sturdy, practical tools and, if you will, a handy chair for a bit of rest after an hour in the sun or when the day's labor is ended. Thus, to real gardeners, the toolhouse is a place of revealing truths and symptoms, as here at the home of Mr. and Mrs. Willard Downing of New Canaan, Connecticut.

Flowers

Let a thousand flowers bloom. Without them, life, and art, would be quite barren. Flowers loom large in mythology, in folklore, in ritual. They stand for houses and dynasties and thrones, countries and chivalries, love and loss, life and death. So much human effort and aspiration and beauty and sadness are embodied in the passing arrangement of petals on a stem that it's impossible to conceive of life at all without the metaphor of bud and blossom, much less the real thing.

America may be a latecomer to the botany of desire, but it has caught up quickly with its domesticating urge. Americans are cultivators. Much of this country's florabundance is indigenous. Perhaps an equal number of species has been imported for scientific as well as for scenic purposes. Only a century ago this country was in the process of paving its way from an agrarian to an industrial economy. Flowers were a luxury, an accident, or a weed. Now they are a global industry.

American design and decoration have developed from the outside in, through a process of cross-pollination. We have consistently imported fashions and ideas, especially those that relate to connoisseurship, and assimilated them into the arts of appreciation that we use to distinguish living well from just living. Floral design is one of the minor arts for which Americans have hardly had sufficient leisure—or sufficient crop-free land—until relatively recently. By the close of the Victorian era, Americans were beginning to use flowers and floral arrangements, such as the nosegay, to complete the décor of their interiors. With the rise of Art Nouveau, single-stem vases or those with just a few stems were deemed appropriate in elegant households. Profusion went the way of the crinoline.

By the 1930s, American hostesses were beginning to develop a passion for the floral centerpiece as a formal element of the dining table décor. As the shelter magazines began to devote an increasing number of pages to educating their readers about how to dress the table for different celebrations and events, they provided advice on how to organize, select, arrange, and present the most suitable display for the particular room and

The 1980s were the decade of hot art and David Salle was among the hottest of the decade's artists. The sense that artists could be players in the high-stakes games of the boom period is perfectly expressed in Salle's loft—a highly designed space filled with the best of 1950s furniture. To drive the point home, the pictures were taken by no less a person than Robert Mapplethorpe, then the hottest photographer on the planet.

the specific event. As floral fashions changed, they kept readers up to date on the arrangements of the hour—how to accessorize them, and when to use silk. A healthy dose of the American competitive spirit fertilizes the attitude that American gardeners have toward their favorite flowers. With the dawn of the garden club and the rise of the flower show in the early part of the twentieth century, the ladies and gentlemen of the American suburb began to engage in the first form of pitched coed battle this country had ever seen. While participants may face off bloodlessly, sap is certainly let. Tactics have been fierce, made no less brutal by the exquisite nature of the weapons—and by the enforced politesse of the rules of engagement and the strict adherence to the trial by jury system of judging the better, bigger, more ostentatious bloom.

Nature has always been a primary inspiration for an element of pattern, as well as for color palette. Blooms of all kinds are integral to the decorative arts tradition. We can often recognize an artist or an architect, or at least the period in which he or she worked, by the way and the degree to which he or she has abstracted or finessed the components of stem, petal, leaf, stamen, and sepal into a language of pattern and ornament. What would a Dorothy Draper interior of the mid-century be without its cabbage roses? Or a William Morris hand-blocked paper without its irises and peacock feathers? Or the Adams brothers without their acanthus leaves? It's hard to think of Marimekko without picturing Unikko, the perennially popular print based on the bold blowsy blossom of papaver orientalis.

Horticulture is a fascination (or obsession) for many Americans. This, after all, is a country in which each state has its own flower. Throughout the decades, gardens, trees, and flowers have been the subjects of some of the twentieth century's most remarkable photographs and greatest paintings. While exquisite solitary blooms have lost some of their popularity as floral displays, close-up photographs of botanical specimens, from hothouse tropical plants to water lilies to desert succulents, have never gone out of style in our homes or in our magazines. Flowers, after all, provide a perennial reminder that hope really does spring eternal, even if the bloom goes off every rose eventually.

According to Fleeta Brownell Woodroffe, a garden enthusiast and writer who took this photo of H. P. Sass with his Hesperus plants in 1940, blooming daylilies save us from the garden's July slump—that period between the high tide of roses, peonies, Canterbury bells, and delphiniums and the fall carpet of asters and mums. Her article, "Great Daylilies Ahead," identified hybridizers of new species and showed them with their blooms. Sass was a legendary American plant breeder, and a charter member of the American Iris Society.

One of the first rounds that children learn to sing is about white coral bells upon their slender stalks, like these photographed by Coppi Barbieri in 2000. The little flowers of the lily of the valley emit a delicious scent that has inspired at least one perfume. Sweetness doesn't come without a price, however: every part of this little lily is toxic.

Pages 158-159: Most water plants require little care, and are almost weedlike in their vigor. The pickerel rush in particular is a hardy plant, which can be left outdoors in northern zones. More tender varieties, such as taro, should be brought indoors for the winter. In 1999 Todd Eberle photographed this pickerel rush, *Pontederia cordata*, a robust pondside perennial that blooms freely all summer.

Right: A rose by any other name might smell as sweet as an orange, as Dana Gallagher's photograph, taken in 2000, suggests. That's exactly the case with the 'Sonia Rykiel,' which infuses the garden with the scent of citrus. The blooms of this variety open to reveal golden centers. The shrub grows to approximately 3 to 4 feet.

The lotus is a much storied flower, with a place in the spiritual and literary traditions of cultures as diverse as Chinese, Indian, Egyptian, Irish, and Greek. Homer and Joyce have their lotus eaters, and Buddha sits on the lotus throne, a symbol of faithfulness and enlightenment. Fernando Bengoechea photographed this single stem in 1997. It was one of numerous exotic plants that the late landscape architect Pietro Porcinai had used to transform a formal Italian Renaissance garden into a tropical shrine.

Todd Eberle photographed the lotus 'Nelumbo,' commonly called 'Carolina Queen,' in 1999. She is a giant of the water garden, and can easily grow to a height of six feet. The tropical lotuses hold their showy blooms above the waterline, like proper ladies who don't want to ruin their hairdos while swimming.

In addition to being one of the twentieth century's great photographers, Edward Steichen was also a celebrated breeder of delphiniums, a passion that he wrote about in *House & Garden* in 1932, the year before the magazine published this slightly surreal photograph of a young woman amid delphinium spires. In 1936, he persuaded the Museum of Modern Art to put up a show of his flowers, the first in which MoMA gave living things the same status as man-made objects. "Without this sustenance," Steichen later wrote, "I don't believe I could have remained alive and interested in my professional photographic activities in New York for as long as I did." In 1938, he closed his studio, exchanging his reputation as the highest-paid photographer for a quieter renown in botany circles.

There is far more to the tulip than meets the eye. This flower came to the West along the Silk Route, and was the cause of the world's first case of irrational exuberance in the financial market. Tulipmania indeed. The graceful blooms—and their reflections in an antique mirror—capture the subtle palette of the room that they adorn. The photograph was taken by Thibault Jeanson in 2000.

Michael T. McDermit photographed the bowing blossoms of the hybrid musk rose 'Cornelia' after a 2001 rain at Roseraie de Berty, one of the most respected Old Rose nurseries in France. Hidden in the rugged, mountainous terrain of the Ardeche, the nursery harbors nearly 600 varieties of Old Roses in its nooks and crannies.

Above: Melanie Acevedo took this photograph of flower power in 2000. The wall covering is linen printed with a sunflower pattern. The bouquet painted on the vase includes lilies, roses, and tulips. The live riot of purple is hydrangeas. The masterminds behind this color extravaganza are designers William Diamond and Anthony Baratta.

Right: This study in the power of primary colors poses red and yellow striped parrot tulips in elegant Chinese blue-and-white vases that are old, but not so rare that they can't be used for flowers. Melanie Acevedo photographed this still life on a drawing room table in 2001.

Photographed by Matthew Benson in 2000, these water lilies float in a pool in a sunken garden in Greenwich, Connecticut, created by opinionated English landscape designer Simon Johnson. Johnson imposed English style and substance on this New England estate, organizing the spaces with a clear, crisp symmetry infused with a restrained romanticism.

Bonsai creates living poetry with nature's elements. This leafy haiku, photographed by Carlton Davis in 2001, is a dwarf boxwood cultivated in the ishitsuki style and rooted on a cliff-like stone. This particular type of bonsai is often placed in a dish of shallow water to create a reflection.

Although he is known for photographs closely allied with his progressive politics—of protests, working men and women, cityscapes—Paul Strand also produced a body of work inspired by the natural world, like this 1937 picture of the leaves of the mullein plant, the first in a series he did for the magazine. The modesty of his weedy subject, the intensity of feeling in the picture, and its insistent objectivity are Strand hallmarks, as central here as they are in his political work.

Entertaining

America is the nation of the open door. We pride ourselves on our capacity for welcome. Come on in, we say. Join us, we suggest. So it has been, here, in this land of immigrants, since the Pilgrims debarked at Plymouth Rock, gave thanks, and made their distinctly grave sort of whoopee. The nation's first tea party was something of a democratic, if mostly male, affair. The country-at-large was invited to pursue life, liberty, and happiness through insurrection—and almost everyone pitched in.

Entertaining is as much about exclusion as it is about inclusion. Hence the age-old device of the A-list, which seems to have emerged in America during the increasing prosperity of the second half of the nineteenth century. Thank Mrs. Astor for elevating the "s" in Society, by naming and framing her world with the 400—the de facto New York Knickerbockers, descendants of the city's founding families.

Here's to the age of innocence and the house of mirth. To produce a party on the scale of one of Mrs. Stuyvesant Fish's legendary affairs requires more than just a single pair of hands. Clearly, hostesses at the turn of the twentieth century had the kind of domestic staff beyond imagining today.

After World War I, going into service began to lose its appeal as a first career for new immigrants and others. With the dawn of the Jazz Age, formerly segregated circles, the various "our" crowds, started to intermingle with one another rather freely over gin and other high spirits—certainly the cocktail has always helped to liquidate existing social barriers. By the 1930s American magazines were documenting the disappearance of the professional servant, a situation that heralded the arrival of a new domestic reality—one that nudged the hostess herself back into the kitchen.

The buffet offers a very specific example of how each generation resurrects useful conventions from the past and adapts them to serve the present. The reinvention of this old-fashioned form of entertaining after World War II reflects the fact that party giving in America was changing as progressively more women entered the

Whether you're on a polo pony or just cheering from the sidelines, after a few chukkers, you're bound to be hungry. Such a tony pastime might seem to call for an open-air dinner complete with butler, but in a democratic nation, a tailgate party is just the thing. Still, in such a venue, it shouldn't be too down-market. A 1964 article on "Take-Along Shelters" instructed readers on creating everything from gazebos to tailgate tents. Here, in Rudy Müller's photograph, a sporty striped awning helps turn a station wagon into a smart buffet table. Everything is in order, and there is enough food to choke a horse—not literally, of course.

workplace, and as the availability of household staff became essentially obsolete. From their infancy, shelter magazines had addressed the subject of domestic help and acknowledged the upstairs/downstairs division of labor in the American home. The comeback of the buffet provided a way to entertain elegantly and easily, with or without hired help. It also offered, and continues to present, an opportunity for the host or hostess to experiment with the delights of décor on the small scale of the tabletop.

During the twentieth century, the metronome of manners swung regularly between formal and informal, although the parameters of formality and informality have changed over time and with fashion, as well as upon reflection. Casual style and the do-it-yourself spirit reigned during the war years and the decade thereafter, but by the late 1950s some were begging for a return to a more dressy and ceremonial approach to entertaining, which did in fact arrive with youthful flourish during the Camelot years of the early 1960s. By the end of that tempestuous decade, the tables had turned yet again. The urbane Billy Baldwin noted in 1971: "Not so many years ago, the dining room was the ultimate in pomp and circumstance. Today, thank goodness, we are more concerned with the personal in entertaining than perfection."

We are a nation of eaters, as well as a nation of immigrants. Food means much to us. It represents culture and heritage, as well as the appreciation of the variety of the world beyond our admittedly wide borders. In the last half-century, Americans have become obsessed with ingredients and cuisine. We have started growing our own foodstuffs, as we did early in the century. Today, America delights in gastronomical adventure—and in sharing the wealth of those experiences with friends both old and new.

Fashions change in entertaining, as they do in everything else in life, but manners remain at heart the same. Etiquette, after all, is diplomacy practiced on the home front. Manners are essential because they smooth the ways of human congress. The specific gestures may wax and wane, and the precise details of polite behavior may vary from place to place and from culture to culture, but "welcome," "please," and "thank you" are the words and the attitudes that we respect above most others—and in which we train our children from the time they can say "more."

Entertaining is an art form that is private in its labors and public in its performance, preferably as nonchalant as possible. As Elsie de Wolfe, the late Lady Mendl, once wrote, "I never jump up from my chair, leave the room, or run up and downstairs after my guests arrive. But I work like an army of rabbits before they come." She had servants. We most likely don't. But the preparation necessary for the pleasure to come is comparable. That's entertaining. So let's party.

A chic couple prepares for a dockside clambake, a breeze to pull off, thanks to the new accessories of the "portable age"—folding tables and chairs, freezer packs, plastic bags and aluminum foil—documented by John Rawlings in 1952. All this convenience, including frozen food, does not preclude the handmade touch, an embroidered Mexican cloth.

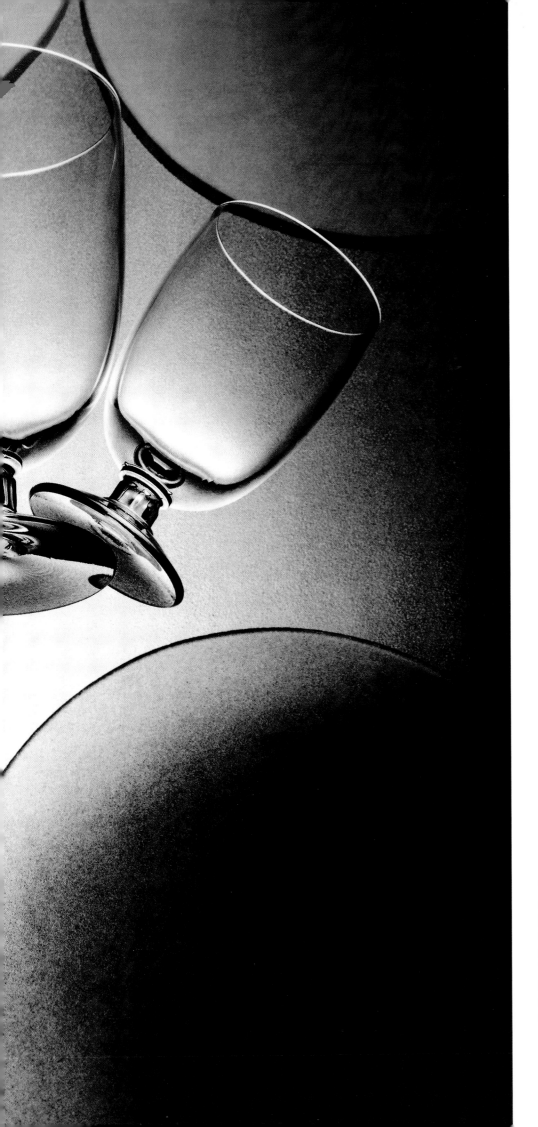

There's nothing like an impending marriage to set off a flurry of parties, including one just for the bride. Obviously, the table must be decorated for the occasion. This still life of glass goblets and plates photographed by Anton Bruehl in 1936 suggests a few sparkling possibilities.

Above: As Bernard Devoto, the American historian and critic, wrote in *Harper's* in 1949, "You can no more keep a martini in the refrigerator than you can keep a kiss there. The proper union of gin and vermouth is one of the happiest marriages on earth, and one of the shortest-lived." While the days of the three-martini lunch are gone, the most elegant of cocktails retains its state of grace—and this 2001 photograph by Don Forbes shows why.

Right: At a loss for an unusual setting for a party table? Try a still life in glass for a centerpiece, as "Glass: Dancing Lights for Party Tables," a 1965 article on the versatility of one of our oldest materials, suggested. The tabletop caught by Rudy Müller's camera blooms with jewel tones.

Page 188: The cover of *House & Garden's* May 1949 bridal issue featured a Horst P. Horst photograph of a smartly dressed young bride preparing for a dinner party at her new home. Suggestions for achieving high style on a newlywed's budget included using denim for curtains and cushions, outdoor furniture in the dining room, and rubber tiles on the floor. By contrast, the silver flatware is from Georg Jensen. Inside the issue, readers eager for information could pick up tips on menus, the etiquette of entertaining, table settings, and wedding gifts that last, as well as gardening advice and a look at the fresh ideas about living that were cropping up in the designs of America's new modern houses.

Page 189: There is much to be said for the entertainment value of discovering the Platonic ideal of something, such as Ladurée's macaroons, the ne plus ultra of this particular confection. Then, of course, you have to do your best to share your discovery with friends. Ilan Rubin's 1996 photo documents the heart and soul of this obsession with perfection and consumption.

Right: When the urge to merge with the Caribbean strikes, but a trip to the islands is out of the question, exercise a little creativity and paint a backyard paradise. That, at least, is what the caption to this 1955 photograph by John Rawlings advised: "To be truly authentic serve rum cocktails, chilled avocado soup, chicken broiled outdoors, Antilles style, and have a stack of calypso records on the hi-fi." Valerian Rybar designed the centerpiece of shells and brilliant blue butterflies.

Tents and parties go together like, well, couscous and tajine. But pitching a traditional Berber chieftain's tent on the rooftop of your getaway house in Tangiers adds another level of romance to candlelight dining beneath the sheltering sky. "There is something irresistible about a tent," says its owner, Yves Vidal. "No one wants to leave it." For the Berbers, the carpeted "caidale," as this kind of tent is called, represents generosity. Like the spirit it describes in David Massey's 1972 photograph, a tent can travel with you anywhere.

Left: Anton Bruehl's 1937 photograph captures a moment in time when drinking foamy eggnog, eating Virginia ham and biscuits, and smoking at the cocktail table were not only acceptable but also sophisticated forms of behavior. Holiday revelry just isn't what it used to be.

Right: As Jay McInerney wrote in his wine column in 1996, "Upon first tasting the sparkling wine of Champagne, Dom Perignon is said to have called out to a fellow friar, 'Come quickly, I'm tasting stars.' Apocryphal or not, this is surely one of the best descriptions in the history of wine commentary." It's also true that nothing hollers "party" more convincingly than a champagne bottle. And nothing is more evocative of champagne, and therefore of celebration, than a cluster of corks left overat the end of a particularly festive affair. Ilan Rubin's photograph of this sculptural stack of champagne stoppers practically sings with the sharp sound that accompanies the release of compressed corks as they pop magnificently from their heavy bottles.

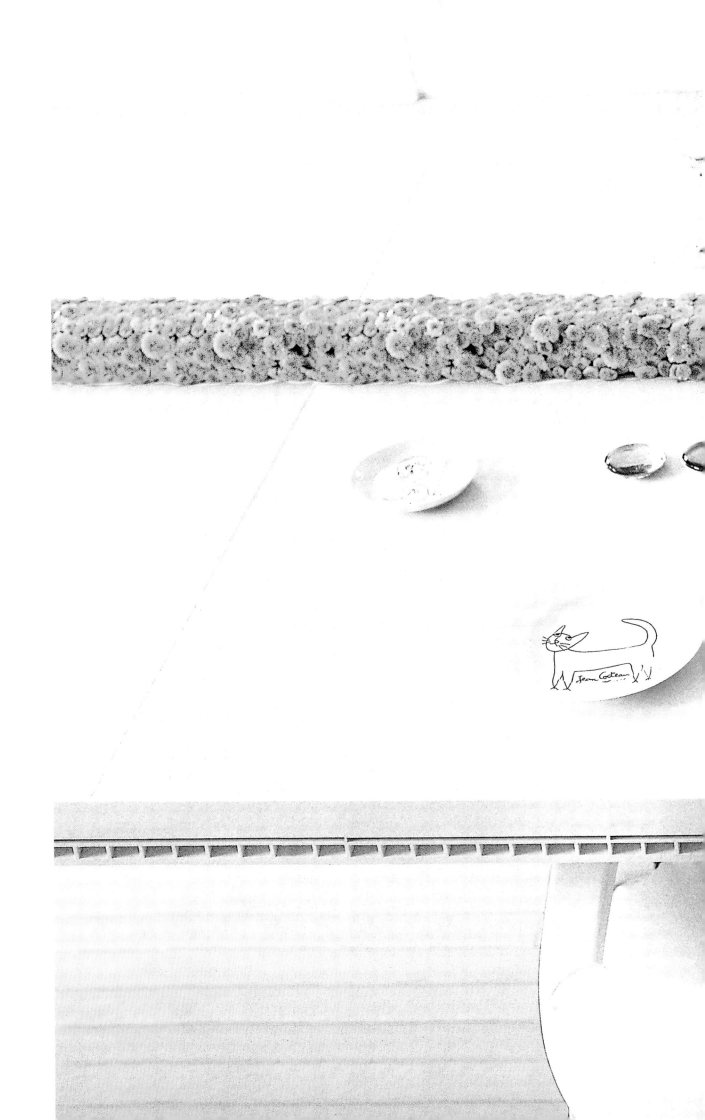

Pages 196-197: A centerpiece made of chrysanthemums embedded in Styrofoam blocks adds color to a predominantly white table in Judith Niedermaier's luminous, almost all-white apartment in Chicago. Low enough to leave an unobstructed view of fellow guests across the table, surreal enough to match the spirit of the Jean Cocteau drawings on the china, and minimalist enough to mirror the décor, this Maginot Line of mums stretches across the central portion of the tabletop without eating up too much space. William Abranowicz's 1999 photograph emphasizes the dreamy quality of the dining room, which makes guests feel "as if they are floating through the heavens."

Right: Presentation matters. And garnishes can make a meal, as this so-called Harlequin Chicken, an "op-art study" shot by Ernst Beadle in 1964, shows. How to do it? Coat the bird with chaufroid sauce, then pattern the surface with diamond-shaped pieces of eggplant skin. The rosettes are whittled from raw turnips.

Horst P. Horst photographed this still
life, which was composed with
the sand, sun, and sea in mind.
It accompanied two 1949 articles
on the pleasures of summer, among
them music festivals around the
country and wine coolers that take
the heat off sultry afternoons.

Above: In a topsy-turvy world, dessert would always come first. That's the kind of world that children want, and many adults, too. Hence cookbook author Gail Monaghan's search to re-create the lost desserts of her childhood, of which the Brown Derby's orange chiffon cake is one. This California classic embodies the high hopes of its era, and the rich fruitiness of its geography. For Monaghan, who grew up in Beverly Hills, a swell time out in childhood involved ordering more than one of the opulent desserts on the menu of Chasens, say, or the Brown Derby, or Scandia. Searching for those moments that sweeten her memory, Monaghan asks herself after each attempt not so much "Is this the taste I remember?" but "Is this the experience?"

Right: As re-created by Gail Monaghan and photographed by Ilan Rubin in 2001, the Scandia Danish torte has all the glamour of the 1950s original.

Ogden Nash wrote a poem,
"How to Hitchcock," to accompany a droll
series of photos that John Rawlings
snapped in 1956 at "21," the New York
hot spot, of an impish Alfred Hitchcock
carving a Christmas turkey.
Nash's ditty read in part:
"Pick a Hitchcock of opulence rather
than corpulence, / Just pleasingly plump,
with a snug silhouette, / To embellish
the board when the places are set.
/ For the ultimate test, more closely
examine it. / The Hitchcock supreme
has a wide streak of ham in it."

In 1952, Clifford Coffin photographed dining room styles in tropical settings, including this covered veranda where Mr. Odo Cross entertained. Lattice walls frame a dining pavilion that magazine editors called "as gay as a circus tent." The Moorish door opens to an awninged terrace beyond.

Pages 208-209: For a 1947 article entitled "Table Manners: If You Haven't a Maid, Simplify Your Service," Herbert Matter snapped a collage made up of appropriate components for a pass-the-platter dinner party. "Although carving at the table is more or less in the discard," wrote the editors, "food is often served by the hostess from her place at the table. (Casserole dishes, now so popular, are ideal for this.)"

Right: In war-ravaged Europe, people still didn't have enough to eat, while Americans scuttled 125 million pounds of food in a day. Freedom and food, the magazine said in 1948, "are too precious to waste." Irving Penn's stark photograph—all the more powerful because it is in black and white— of an empty table and a plate scraped clean symbolizes a hungry continent.

Home Away from Home

There is always another frontier. Pioneers of every stripe built the United States, and no sooner had many of them constructed a house than they dreamed of another, a place far removed, stylistically at least, from their daily routines. In the early twentieth century, vacation outposts tended to resemble fortresses and bunkers—vestiges of a time when settlers were often under siege. For those who wanted the luxury of roughing it, turn-of-the-century architects constructed log cabin fantasies and ranch revivals—and filled them with all the era's mod cons.

In the expanding middle classes at the past century's dawn, vacating the city for the summer was as much a matter of health as of pleasure. Americans, after all, have tended to follow Juvenal's proposition that sound minds dwell in sound bodies. For those less well off than the gilded class, the dream getaway might be a cabin, a beach shack, or a houseboat—or an early-twentieth-century version of a mobile home. From the beginning, shelter magazines covered these more modest second homes, as well as the various country "camps" and waterfront "cottages" of the wealthy. In "The Portable House," for example, which ran in *House & Garden* in 1906, Boston-based writer Livingston Wright noted that "in many a country community it is not a safe thing to leave a summer-house uncared for during the long winter." But, he continued, "with your portable—why, the thing don't cost much, and if you want to go away, why you just—take your house right to pieces and pack it up just as you do your trunk." Wright ended the article with a price list: buyers could get a 10 ft. by 10 ft. room for $100; two additional rooms of the same size, $80; a 10 ft. by 10 ft. screened room, $80; a side porch with an awning, $30; one "L"-hinged room, $35. The grand total for the little getaway came to $450—roughly $24,000 today. By the late 1920s, Americans had taken to the road in droves. As travel got easier and safer, and wild places were made tame, the architecture of secondary residences began to reflect the carefree spirit of a nation of go-getters. Vacation places ran a stylistic gamut from simple to extravagant: the A-frames, log cabins, sheds, bungalows, haciendas, and even palatial "cottages" for weekends, holidays, and summers were designed to blend with the surrounding landscape. Panoramic decks and oversized porches commanded spectacular views. The décor of

In 1971, Finnish design was all the rage, and architect Matti Suuronen's lightweight molded fiberglass house, by Polykem, photographed by John Cowan, makes clear why. You could live in one room, hook rooms together, or stack them. The first-floor skylight converted to an opening for a spiral stair.

these country and beach houses was often relaxed and playful, whether French Provincial, Anglo-colonial wicker, or American twig. A breezy spirit of rustic comfort, always popular in the kind of homes away from home that American consumers either owned or aspired to, became increasingly popular.

Americans have always treasured their leisure because it has almost always been so hard won. The fight to flight has long been part of the American attitude toward the weekend. After the Second World War, as working life in America seemed to pick up speed and gain complexity, the need to reacquaint oneself and one's family with the simple pleasures reasserted itself, in the process inspiring another wave of Americans to find their homes away from home. As the nation prospered, the country went on something of a building spree and certainly on a baby boom. The contemporary houses of the mid-century, many of them vacation homes, featured free-flowing interior spaces, minimal forms, lightweight furniture, and the kind of relaxed aesthetic that can be swept clear of tracked-in dirt or sand from the beach without much trouble. This style of living became synonymous with modernity—an aesthetic, and a way of existence, that has enjoyed a second coming in recent years.

Each generation of Americans has discovered for itself, in its own way, the deep sigh of relief that comes upon crossing the threshold of the home away from home—wherever it may be. Many people try to resettle in the summer places of their youth. Some find their second homes much farther afield. Still others stick to the weekend commuter's golden rule. And there will always be those who are at home, away from home, on the road. The point of getting away is the arrival at a place that may be home, but where the living is actually easy—or at least where it can be. The home away from home is the promise of the good life, and the object of the American dream.

Ezra Stoller photographed this residence in 1963. The house, which was designed by California architects Thornton Ladd and John Kelsey, has a cantilevered terrace that thrusts out over the water like a ship's prow—and that's supported by tall concrete piers planted into the face of the cliff. The conversation circle, with a cushioned terrazzo shelf curving around a fire pit that's centered in a dark concrete slab, is shielded from winds and sea spray by a high glass fence.

Above: Mr. and Mrs. Alfred Rose summered at Lake Placid, on an island accessible only by boat, in a house designed by Robert Allan Jacobs. Robert M. Damora photographed the place in the height of summer 1949. The house itself is smaller than this airy porch and pier suggest. According to the magazine editors, "Since it was impossible to get materials for rebuilding at that time, Mr. Jacobs suggested they remodel the boat house instead. As it turned out, the Roses like the house so well that they have dropped all plans for a larger place and say they never want a big house again." The dimensions of the living space? 32 ft. by 70 ft.

Left: Instead of siting this weekend retreat on top of a hill overlooking the Tennessee River near Shiloh, architect Coleman Coker built it into the cliff. The unusual steel railing he designed for the deck is one of the elements that give the place its fitting mix of rusticity and contemporary design. François Dischinger photographed the house in 2000.

Page 218: In 1998, Kurt Markus photographed and wrote about his family's woody retreat on Flathead Lake in Montana. His caption for this image read, "Weston, fourteen, does all the yard work. His reward: relaxing in the hammock, while Bo finds some shade."

Page 219: Mark and Debbie Callaway built a Florida beach house with a yacht-like interior, complete with snug bunks and a bolted-down dining table. Photographed in 1998 by François Dischinger, the house has dark-mahogany ceilings and antique heart-pine floors. Teak unifies elements of the house, and helps to give it its seagoing flavor. Gabriella Callaway rinses off in the shower room on the back porch, which has a teak floor.

Right: Designer Gaston Berthelot, a Frenchman living in New York City, built a vacation retreat overlooking the Mediterranean, near the village of Hammamet in Tunisia. Photographed by David Massey in 1970, the house combines traditional building techniques (stucco-covered stone walls, for example) with modern conveniences. "Guidebooks tell you," says Berthelot, "that life in Tunisia is magical and exotic. But even more it's as relaxing as anything I've ever found, and that's why I like it."

Robert Polidori photographed this machine for capturing mountain views in 2000. The Y house, as it's known, was designed by architect Steven Holl as a Catskill getaway for clients who like their solitude. The living room, with a giant deck, is on the left, over the guest bedrooms. The other arm of the house includes the master bedroom, which is positioned above the kitchen and dining room.

223

The Beach Boys weren't even the Beach Babies yet, but southern California was already looking like a happening place. Fred R. Dapprich's 1940 photograph of a Las Tunas Beach house illuminates the combination of casual (though hard-edged) informality and limitless horizon, complete with surf, that was beginning to make hearts race.

Above: Julius Shulman photographed architect Albert Frey's one room, 16-foot by 20-foot house in Palm Springs in 1948. The limited living spaces, however, extend to the outdoors. One wing wall goes beyond the living area to divide the barbecue and pool terraces. Frey put cushions covered in bright colors on the poolside seats of poured concrete.

Page 226: Michel Arnaud's 1998 photograph of the beach through the dark blue glass of an Archimede Seguso vase is a clever piece of trompe l'œil, indicating how closely allied in spirit this residence is to the South Carolina beach outside its walls. "People here can get a little worried that their objects are exposed to sunlight, that their things are going to fade," says owner David Rawle. "What if my things are fading? I'm fading, too."

Page 227: Sculptor and painter Sandro Chia was photographed in 1999 by Melanie Acevedo as he rode one of his vintage motorcycles up the cypress-lined drive to Castello Romitorio, his Tuscan retreat. The medieval castle is nestled in the Sienese hills, and surrounded by vineyards.

Pages 228-229: The home of Mr. and Mrs. Georges Sebastian in Hammamet on the North African coast, photographed in 1934 by George Hoyningen-Huene, stands in a white walled garden above a dusty, cactus-hedged road. All the walls were whitewashed. Designed by its owners, the house was equipped for both summer and winter, and furnished with the designs of Jean-Michel Frank and Eyre de Lanux.

Above: Edward Steichen took this wintry photograph of his house in New England in 1944, while he was still in the service. "Set unobtrusively on a typical New England country hillside," wrote the editors, "the home of Lieut. Comdr. Steichen exemplifies successful individualism in design. The owner is an admirer of the open plan—in fact, his architect believes he would have preferred to build the house as one large room, had that been practicable." The architect in question was the firm of Evans, Moore and Woodbridge of New York.

Right: Art Hupy photographed this hexagonal getaway in the Rockies outside Aspen, Colorado, in 1963. Built as a family sanctuary, as well as headquarters for supervising the summer grazing of a herd of beef cattle, the house is without telephone or electricity. Designed by architect Fredric Benedict, the relatively inexpensive house ($10,000) has rough-sawn spruce siding, a weathered redwood deck, and a roof of redwood shakes.

At the Chicago World's Fair of 1933, Eugene Hutchinson photographed America's first glass house, which the magazine's editors called "revolutionary in design and construction." Designed by architect George Fred Keck, and formally known as the "House of Tomorrow," the circular structure was constructed of glass and steel around a spiral staircase that encloses the electrical, plumbing, and air-conditioning systems. On the ground floor were an airplane hanger and garage, hall, heating and cooling unit room, laundry, and rec room. The second floor contained the living spaces. The third floor consisted of a circular sunroom surrounded by an observation terrace. "No windows open," explained the editors, "the air-conditioning system keeping the atmosphere as fresh as a day in June."

François Dischinger photographed the interior of this shipshape Florida beach home in 1998. The children live like elegant sailors, with mahogany bunk beds, drawers, rails, and ladders. They can stow their toys in compartments underneath the floor.

In Hollywood, power
is relative—and visible
in the size of one's trailer.
In 1997 Todd Eberle
photographed the interior
of producer Joel Silver's
custom-fitted mobile
stronghold, which was
designed by Thierry Despont.
The interior is nothing if not
streamlined, with vintage
1940s chairs and coffee table
by Warren McArthur and a
sofa by Paul T. Frankl.

In the rigorously conventional 1950s, the magazine proclaimed, "For a free and easy summer, make your living portable." Portability translated into both spontaneity and practicality: two half shells, photographed in 1957 by Lois and Joe Steinmetz, were dandy windscreens on the beach. Put together, they were a boat. Very crafty.

Acknowledgments

This book is the result of one magazine's long love affair with the pleasures of home. Its debt is to a hundred years of writers, editors, and photographers who have contributed to its pages. For their work in putting this passion between hardcovers, we wish to thank: Philip Reiser, Charles Scheips, Anthony Jazzar, Lucy Gilmour, Elizabeth Pochoda, Katrine Ames, Alice Siempelkamp, and Judith Nasatir. For their encouragement we are indebted to Si Newhouse, James Truman, Steve Florio, and Chuck Townsend.

House & Garden

April 1926 · Interior Decoration Number

House & Garden

Double Number · APRIL 1940

CONDÉ NAST

House & Garden

NOVEMBER 1997

Creature Comforts

10 Heavenly Wing Chairs
Victoriana Revisited
L.A. Rediscovered
High Drama Table Settings

House & Garden

19 Steps to Building a House

Inside News – Easy Modern

February 1946 · Price 35 Cents

HOUSE & GARDEN

IDEAL HOUSE OF 1938
SPRING DECORATING REVIEW

House & Garden

August · 1921 · Household Equipment Number

House & Garden

HOUSES AND PLANS

When is a Small House large?
A Cantilevered House

August 1947 Price 35 Cents

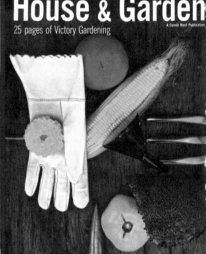

House & Garden

25 pages of Victory Gardening

JANUARY 1944 · PRICE 35 CENTS

HOUSE & GARDEN

CAREFREE EUROPEAN STYLE

CONDÉ NAST

House & Garden

Silver Season

Glow in Los Angeles
Sparkle in New York
Bright Gift Ideas

DECEMBER 1996

HOUSE & GARDEN

A Condé Nast Publication

Remodeling Number · November, 1934 · Price 35 Cents

HOUSE & GARDEN

THE MAGAZINE OF CREATIVE LIVING

JANUARY 1964

House & Garden

COLOR STORY
SPRING SHOPPING GUIDE
SPRING GARDENING

House & Garden

A Condé Nast Publication

Spring Gardening

On Your Own
First Flights in Decoration

May 1945
Price 35 Cents

House & Garden

SINCE 1901

NEW YORK NOW

HOW A NEW GENERATION DECORATES

JUNE 2000

House & Garden

LIVE AS WELL
AS YOU LOOK